MW01057644

ONE GOD ...

OR THREE?

ONE GOD...
OR THREE?

Exploring the Tri-Unity
of God
In the Old Testament

by

STANLEY ROSENTHAL

THE SPEARHEAD PRESS
Publishing Division of
THE FRIENDS OF ISRAEL GOSPEL MINISTRY, INC.
West Collingswood, N.J. 08107

ONE GOD . . .
OR THREE?

Copyright © 1978

The Friends of Israel Gospel Ministry, Inc.
West Collingswood, N.J. 08107

First Edition 1978

All rights reserved

ISBN O-87508-464-8

This edition by special arrangement.

Published by Christian Literature Crusade, Inc.
Fort Washington, Pennsylvania 19034 USA

Printed in U.S.A.

D E D I C A T E D

To Those Remarkable People . . . . . .

"Who are the Israelites . . . to whom
pertaineth the adoption, and the glory,
and the covenants, and the giving of the law,
and the service of God, and the promises; Whose are
the fathers, and of whom as concerning the
flesh, Messiah came, who is over all.
God blessed for ever."

With my fervent prayer that they
might recognize Him today.

TABLE OF CONTENTS

INTRODUCTION

INTRODUCTION

It is safe to say that most Christians would be at a loss to explain the biblical doctrine of the trinity of God. It is a concept universally rejected by Jews as a contradiction to the monotheistic teaching (the doctrine that there is but one God) found in the Old Testament. Judaism maintains, and properly so, that God has specifically instructed — even commanded — the Jewish people to refuse any rival deities. The history of Israel is replete with the stern consequences the nation suffered when this restriction against idolatry was violated. Indeed, the basic theme of the Torah (the five books of Moses) is the doctrine of the unity of God. To the Jewish mind, therefore, a triune God is totally inconsistent with this teaching.

Before beginning the examination of the subject at hand, one important consideration should be brought to our attention. Because we do not comprehend all sides of a divinely stated truth, we must not therefore reject it as unacceptable. Those who believe in God are faced with many statements concerning His attributes which are not fully understood. In some instances, this is explained by the fact that as finite human beings, we have no capacity to experience these attributes personally. Nevertheless, we accept them as true because we place our faith in what the Scriptures say.

A clear illustration of this may be seen in the Bible's teaching which declares God to be *omnipresent* — everywhere at the same time; *omniscient* — knowing all things; and *omnipotent* — the all-powerful, almighty One. It also speaks of His *eternality* — not only will He go on forever, but He always was — He has no beginning, Admittedly, these concepts go far beyond our abilities of intellectual assimilation, yet there seems to be no problem in our accepting these qualities of God.

Most of us readily acknowledge our limitations in this area. In fact, we see it as quite consistent with the nature of God as supreme, and of humanity as mortal. If it were possible to fully comprehend God, we would have succeeded in reducing Him to no more than a human being; or we would have elevated humanity to the position of Deity. Of course, neither of these suggestions is acceptable.

With these preliminary considerations in mind, let us focus attention on the central theme: *God is one, but at the same time consists of three persons, without negating the unity of Jehovah.*

The Tri-Unity of God

Regrettably, for approximately 1,600 years the term trinity has been used to explain the nature of God. Choosing this particular word was as unfortunate as it was incorrect. A wrong choice of words can cause much confusion, as it has done in this instance. When Christians use the term trinity (which simply means three), they unconsciously communicate the concept of polytheism (belief in or worship of a plurality of gods). The word trinity was coined to refer to the plurality of God, and yet maintain the thought of unity. Unfortunately, it was a well-intended but ill-advised choice.

Today, many non-Christians assume that this doctrine means Christendom believes in three gods, not one. At its heart, however, this teaching is really no different than the central Jewish doctrine of the unity of God. To properly understand the true biblical concept of the nature of God, the term *tri-unity* should be used in place of trinity. *Tri-unity* conveys the idea that God is one, but at the same time consists of three persons.

TRI - UNITY

ONE GOD IN THREE PERSONS

Acceptance of this concept does not imply belief in a God who occupies three distinct bodies. Essentially, a person is one who possesses intellect, emotions and will. Therefore, a person may or may not inhabit a body. This is demonstrated in human beings. Humans are persons, and vacating a body of flesh does not make them any less so.

Scripture describes God as a spirit, not inhabiting flesh, yet existing as the Supreme Person. Likewise, angels are spiritual beings, unembodied but possessing attributes of personality. The Bible emphatically teaches that God in *tri-unity* consists of three persons existing in one substance. This in no way indicates a belief in three gods, but rather a belief which is in total agreement with the teachings of the law and the prophets. While it is beyond our ability to experience, or in many respects even to comprehend this phenomenon fully, it is, nonetheless, the biblical position. In order to understand it in any measure, we must turn to the Scriptures with the simple question: What saith the Lord? (All Scripture texts used are taken from The New Scofield Reference Bible.)

THE
COMPOUND
UNITY
OF
GOD

Chapter One

The Compound Unity
of God

THE unity of God is taught throughout the Old Testament. Scores of passages in the law and the prophets converge to provide irrefutable evidence of plurality within the unity of God.

Plurality in the Shema

Jewish people often object to the *tri-unity* of God because of what they believe is taught in the Shema. For most Jewish people, the Shema is the very center of Judaism. It is that foundational passage which is found in the book of Deuteronomy:

"Shema Yisroel Adonai Elohenu Adonai Echad."

Hear, O Israel: The LORD our God *is* one Lord: And thou shalt love the LORD thy God with all thine heart, and with all thy soul, and with all thy might.

Deuteronomy 6:4, 5

The word *Shema* is the first Hebrew word in this passage and means "hear".

The accepted premise among Jewish people views this as saying that God is indivisibly one. Consequently, the objection is raised: I cannot believe in this person, Jesus, whom Christians claim to be God. For them the Shema appears to have silenced forever the argument which embraces the historic Christain belief in the deity of Jesus. However, a careful examination of Deuteronomy 6:4 actually establishes, rather than refutes, the plurality of God. A thorough review of the Hebrew text reveals this beyond any reasonable doubt. Incredibly, the Shema is one of the strongest statements in support of the *tri-unity* of God found in the entire Bible. The very word which allegedly argues against the *tri-unity* of God actually states that God is a plurality. The last word of the Shema is *echad*, which is translated into English as the word "one". This is a compound-unity noun — that is to say, a noun which demonstrates oneness or unity, but at the same time contains several entities. Several examples may be cited.

In Genesis 1:5, Moses used this word when he describes the first day of creation: "And God called the light Day, and the darkness he called Night. And the evening and the morning were the first day." This "one" day or "first" day is the Hebrew word *echad*. The one day referred to consisted of both light and darkness — evening and morning.

In Genesis 2:24, God revealed what was necessary for a happy marriage. He instructs the husband and the wife to become "one flesh", indicating that those two persons should be joined in perfect harmony as a unit. Here again, the word one is *echad*. The point is clear — *echad* is used to indicate oneness in a compound sense.

In Numbers 13, Moses recorded the account of the twelve Hebrew spies sent to view the land of Canaan. As they returned from the mission, according to verse 23, they paused at Eshcol to "cut down . . . a branch with one cluster of grapes . . . ." The word "cluster" is again our word *echad*. Obviously, this single cluster of grapes consisted of more than one grape.

Likewise, in Ezra 2:64, the Bible records: "The whole congregation together was forty and two thousand, three hundred and three score." The words translated "whole congregation" in English are derived from the single Hebrew word *echad*. It is

TWO BECOME ONE FLESH
IN MARRIAGE

obvious that this one congregation was comprised of more than one individual. As a matter of fact, 42,360 Israelites made up the company.

Jeremiah, the Jewish prophet, in chapter 32 of his Spirit-inspired treatise, employs this same word, *echad*, to denote a compound unity. Verses 38 and 39 read: "And they shall be my people, and I will be their God; And I will give them one heart, and one way . . . ." Jeremiah's reference to "one heart" and "one way" encompasses the entire nation of Israel. Again, many are seen as one.

Interestingly, however, there is another Hebrew word which signifies an absolute oneness. That word is *yachid*. In Genesis 22:2, Abraham is told: "Take now thy son, thine *only* son Isaac, whom thou lovest, and get thee into the land of Moriah; and offer him there for a burnt offering . . . ." The term "only" is *yachid*. It is used again in verses 12 and 16 of the same chapter. There is just one son whom God recognizes. Isaac is the son of promise — there is none other. In this sense, *yachid* sets forth absolute singularity — one and only one.

Similarly, in Proverbs 4:3, Solomon

states: "For I was my father's son, tender and *only* beloved in the sight of my mother." In Psalm 22:20, David wrote: "Deliver my soul from the sword; my *only* one from the power of the dog." Also, we find written in Judges 11:34, "And Jephthah came to Mizpeh unto his house, and, behold, his daughter came out to meet him with timbrels and with dances, and she was his *only* child; beside her he had neither son nor daughter." Jeremiah 6:26 states, "O daughter of my people, gird thyself with sackcloth, and wallow thyself in ashes; make thee mourning, as for an *only* son . . . ." And again, in Amos 8:10, ". . . and I will make it like the mourning for an **only** son. . . ." And again in Zechariah 12:10, as God himself is speaking: " . . . and they shall look upon me whom they have pierced, and they shall mourn for him, as one mourneth for his *only* son. . . ."

We see then that the Spirit-inspired penmen of the Bible had two words from which to choose when communicating the truth about the nature of God. It is clear that Jehovah selected the word which identifies Himself as a plurality. The compound-unity noun is always chosen over the absolute singular. The choice of *echad*, instead of *yachid*, leaves no doubt as to what God intended to transmit.

Plurality in the Name of God

In our English Bibles the translators capitalized "g" in God when transmitting the Hebrew words for God — *El* and *Elohim*. In the Hebrew language these words mean "the all-powerful, almighty One."

Both of these nouns are actually the same word. One, however, *El*, is the singular form, while the other, *Elohim*, is plural. Of particular importance is the fact that of the 2,750 times these words are used in the Old Testament, *Elohim*, the plural form, is employed in 2,500 cases.

Exodus, chapter 20 provides an excellent example. In this passage Moses is relaying the Ten Commandments from God to Israel. Jehovah declares, "I am the LORD thy God . . . Thou shalt have no other gods before me" (verses 2, 3). In this statement "God" and "gods" are identical Hebrew words. Both are the word *Elohim*. The variance in translation comes to us because the translators, while giving "gods" its proper plural form, chose in the other case to render *Elohim* in the singular.

Grammatically, it would be equally acceptable to say, "I am the LORD thy Gods . . . Thou shalt have no other gods before me." Thus, this matter of plurality in the name of God should be recognized as a major question which must be reckoned with. Genesis provides a prime illustration. In the account of the creation alone, *Elohim* is used some thirty-two times in reference to God's work in forming the heavens and the earth.

Another instance is found in the Shema. Here the noun "God" is the Hebrew *Elohenu*. *Elohenu* reflects both the plural pronoun "our" God, as well as the plural form *Elohim*.

Again the question is raised: Why would God consistently select the plural form, *Elohim*, to demonstrate His unity? Would not the use of a singular form clearly establish the singular unity concept? The fact is, God chose to communicate, through Moses, the idea of plurality within His unity.

A Point from Genesis

Plurality in personal pronouns, when used in reference to our Lord, lends additional documentation to verify the *tri-unity* of God. Once again we turn to the Genesis record for evidence. Three passages demonstrate the point.

"And God said, Let us make man in our image, after our likeness . . . So God created man in his own image, in the image of God created he him; male and female created he them" (Genesis 1:26, 27).

At the outset one may observe the selection of *Elohim* as the noun form used in the verse; *Elohim* is going to create man. In concert with this choice, the plural personal pronouns "us" and "our" are inserted.

Dr. David L. Cooper makes a valid point, observing that the Hebrew nouns "image" and "likeness" are in the singular person, thus indicating that the speaker and the person spoken to are one in the same. The conclusion is illuminating: Plurality ("us" and "our") is fused with singular terms ("image" and "likeness"), thereby displaying what we might call a unity-in-plurality. Reinforcement is provided by verse 27 when God refers to Himself in the personal singular pronouns "His" and "He".

It must be understood that only God

can create — this is in evidence throughout the Scriptures. Since this is true, who then is referred to in the statement, "Let US make man in OUR image . . . after OUR likeness"? There is only one logical conclusion.

" . . . Behold, the man is become as one of us . . . Therefore the LORD God sent him forth from the garden of Eden . . . " (Genesis 3:22,23). Adam and Eve had transgressed against Jehovah. The divine response was expulsion from the garden of Eden. God observes that since man has "become as one of US . . . " (the personal plural pronoun), he must be ejected.

The third point of emphasis is encountered in the scattering of humanity from before the Tower of Babel. "Come, let us go down, and there confound their language . . . So the LORD scattered them abroad . . . " (Genesis 11:7, 8). Once more, the plural personal pronoun "us" is used, followed by a reference to God — it was "the LORD" who executed the decision, " . . . let US go down".

THE
PROPHETS
CONFIRM
TRI-UNITY

Chapter Two

The Prophets
Confirm Tri-Unity

" THE Old Testament is revealed in the New Testament, and the New Testament is concealed in the Old Testament." As we study the Bible, we are made ever more aware of the accuracy of Augustine's classic comment. Old Testament writers affirm the concept of the compound unity of God; New Testament penmen provide vivid insights into the identity and actions of the members of the Godhead.

Once an understanding of the compound unity of God is established, it is logical to accept the concept of *tri-unity* – God consisting in three persons. Dr. Jacob Gartenhaus has made an enlightening comment about the Old Testament's triune manifestation of God. "The Hebrew Bible abounds with the idea of the three aspects of God: God the incomprehensible; God who appears to man in the image of man; and God who communicates with man by the Holy Spirit."

Father, Son and Holy Spirit

Four major passages found in Isaiah's writings identify three persons within the Godhead. In Chapter 48, verse 12, the prophet records the words of God to Israel: "Hearken unto me, O Jacob and Israel, my called: I am he; I am the first, I also am the last." The Lord continues the theme in verse 16 when He invites them to "Come near unto me, hear this: I have not spoken in secret from the beginning; from the time that it was, there am I; and now the *Lord GOD*, and *his Spirit*, hath sent *me*." One must conclude that the "me" referred to at the end of verse 16 is the speaker, God himself — "the first" and "the last". Two other persons are also presented, "the Lord GOD" and "his Spirit". So we have before us God, His Lord God, and God's Spirit — a *tri-unity*.

Likewise, in Isaiah 42:1 God speaks of His servant, the Messiah: "Behold my *servant,* whom I uphold; mine elect, in whom my soul delighteth; I have put my *Spirit* upon him; he shall bring forth justice to the nations." Here again we see the *tri-unity:* The speaker, God; the servant, Messiah; and the Spirit.

DIAGRAM
Isaiah 48:12-16

v. 12 - "Hearken unto me, O Jacob and Israel, my called: **I am he; I am the first, I am also the last.**"

God is the speaker: The One who has called Israel. "He is the First and the Last."

v. 16 - "Come near unto me, hear this; I have not spoken in secret **from the beginning; from the time that it was there am I**;

God is still the speaker: The "One" from the beginning; the "One" who has always been there ... the "First and the Last."

And now the Lord God, and his Spirit, hath sent me."

sent by

"Me" refers back to the speaker in verses 12 and 16. The "One" from the beginning; "The first and the last" who is **God.** He is shown to be sent by his **Lord God** and **His Spirit.**

Later, the Messiah describes His mission as He says, "The *Spirit* of the *Lord GOD* is upon *me*, because the LORD hath anointed me to preach good tidings unto the meek; he hath sent me to bind up the brokenhearted, to proclaim liberty to the captives, and the opening of the prison to those who are bound" (Isaiah 61:1). He declares that "the *Spirit* of the *Lord GOD* is upon *me* . . . " – *tri-unity* in harmony.

Again we read: "And there shall come forth a rod out of the stem of Jesse, and a *Branch* shall grow out of his roots; And the *Spirit of the LORD* shall rest upon *him* . . . " (Isaiah 11:1, 2). This passage, like those preceding, emphatically projects all three persons of the Godhead: The Lord, the Spirit and the Branch of Jesse (the Messiah).

Father and Son

Complementing Isaiah's references are several which point specifically to the Father and the Son. In Proverbs 30:4, a remarkable question is asked: "Who hath ascended up into heaven, or descended? Who hath gathered the wind in his fists? Who hath bound the waters in a garment?

Who hath established all the ends of the earth? What is his name, and what is his *son's* name, if thou canst tell? The author attests to the fact that the creator of all the earth, God himself, somehow has a Son.

David, in a messianic psalm, declares that the Messiah (the Anointed One) is none other than the Son of God. In this psalm, the Lord and His anointed (Messiah) become the objects of a rebellion raised by the kings of the earth: " . . . the rulers take counsel together, against the *LORD*, and against his *anointed* . . . " (Psalm 2:2). In verse 7, the Lord identifies His Anointed One: "I will declare the decree: The *LORD* hath said unto me, Thou art my *Son*. . . ." The Anointed One is shown to be God's Son. Still further on, in verse 12, men are encouraged to "Kiss the *SON*, lest he be angry, and ye perish from the way, when his wrath is kindled but a little. Blessed are they who put their trust in him." In other words, they are instructed to reverence and pay homage to the Son of God.

Father and Holy Spirit

As Isaiah recounts God's mercies poured upon Israel in chapter 63, verses 8 to 16, he records the fact that God speaks not only of Himself, but also of the Holy Spirit. In verse 10 we read, "But they rebelled, and vexed his *Holy Spirit* . . . ." Verse 11 adds, " . . . Where is he who put his *Holy Spirit* within him?" Verse 14 concludes, " . . . the *Spirit of the LORD* caused him to rest . . . . "

In his penitential prayer recorded in Psalm 51, David alludes to the Holy Spirit when he implores the Father: "Cast me not away from thy presence, and take not thy *Holy Spirit* from me" (verse 11).

The Prophet Zechariah, in chapter 7, verses 7 to 14, describes the spiritual barrenness of contemporary Israel. His warnings to them contain still another specific statement about the Holy Spirit: "Yea, they made their hearts as an adamant stone, lest they should hear the law, and the words which the LORD of hosts hath sent in his *Spirit* by the former prophets . . . " (7:12).

Finally, but not exhaustively, in the first chapter of Genesis we find the Holy Spirit actively participating in the work of creation. The record tells us that God *(Elohim)* was creating the universe, " . . . And the *Spirit of God* moved upon the face of the waters" (1:2). Again the Scripture demonstrates the perfect harmony of the plurality of the Godhead which is bound up in the word *Elohim.*

It would be beneficial to take time to review all Old Testament passages which speak of the Holy Spirit. For those who will invest the time to do so, it will be readily seen that the Holy Spirit, or Spirit of the Lord, is not simply an emanation from God, but rather is One who bears all of the attributes of personality — a person who is an integral manifestation of the tri-une God.

Tri-Unity or Polytheism?

A stark question rises from the pages of the Old Testament: Are we to believe in a God who consists in more than one person, or are we to accept polytheism? A quick review of a few passages will illustrate the alternatives open to us.

In Psalm 45, Israel's king is set forth as God. Specifically, in verses 6 and 7 we read: "Thy throne, O God, is forever and ever; the sceptre of thy kingdom is a right sceptre. Thou lovest righteousness, and hatest wickedness; therefore *God, thy God* hath anointed thee with the oil of gladness above thy fellows." The query must be raised: Who is God's God?

Again in Psalm 110, verse 1, King David says: "The *LORD* said unto *my Lord,* Sit thou at my right hand, until I make thine enemies thy footstool." The question raised here is: Who is David referring to as his Lord? At the time of this writing, David was the king of Israel. There was none greater than David, except God. Who then would be considered David's Lord? To whom was God speaking?

In Genesis 18 and 19, Moses records the destruction of Sodom and Gomorrah. It is evident throughout these chapters that the Lord himself appeared to Abraham as one of the three men who visited him. In verse 24 of chapter 19, we read: "Then the *LORD* rained upon Sodom and upon Gomorrah brimstone and fire from the *LORD* out of heaven." Unquestionably, this reference is identifying two individual persons. Here again the choice is evident: Polytheism or the *tri-unity* of God.

We are certain that the Bible does not teach polytheism. The gulf between *tri-unity* and the concept of many deities is

unspannable. To accuse Christians of believing in three gods is a baseless assertion.
Polytheism projects gods who are independ-
ent entities — gods who consistently act at
cross-purposes with one another. Within the
tri-unity there is always absolute unity in
desire, design and execution. Every biblical
reference shows the Father, Son and Holy
Spirit operating in perfect union. This fact
alone will serve to emphasize the great dif-
ference between the concepts.

JESUS

THE

MESSIAH

IS

GOD

Chapter Three

Jesus the Messiah is God

IT is fundamental that we understand the term "Messiah" as it relates to Jesus Christ. Therefore, before proceeding to an examination of Old Testament Scriptures which teach His deity, a proper definition must be set forth.

We must first see that the word *Christ* is not simply a second name of Jesus. Christ is the English translation of the Greek word *Christos,* which is the Greek translation of the Hebrew term *Messiah.* With respect to this term, the New Testament teaches unequivocally that Jesus is the Messiah, the Anointed One.

Jesus Christ (Jesus, the Messiah) was rejected by His people, the nation Israel — an event foretold by the Prophet Isaiah seven hundred years before His birth. Israel's religious leadership rejected Jesus as their Messiah due to an erroneous concept of Him, causing them to refuse to accept His statements that He was God. In the Gospel of John, chapter 10, verse 30, Jesus

said, "I and my Father are one." His Jewish
hearers were fully aware of what He was
saying. Their reply evidences this: "For a
good work we stone thee not, but for blas-
phemy; and because that thou, being a man,
makest thyself God" (John 10:33). Jesus
counters by saying, "Say ye of him, whom
the Father hath sanctified and sent into the
world, Thou blasphemest; because I said, I
am the Son of God " (verse 36). There is
no question that Jesus and the writers of
the New Testament repeatedly made the
claim that He was both God and Messiah.

The acknowledgment of the deity of
Christ by Bible-believing Christians has,
across the centuries, stood as the central
point of contention which has hindered
Jewish people from accepting Jesus as their
Messiah. It therefore becomes necessary, in
our further exploration of the *tri-unity* of
God, to examine Old Testament proofs that
Messiah, the Anointed One, is not just a
God-empowered figure, but is in truth God.

The Messiah Recognized as God

"For unto us a child is born, unto us
a son is given, and the government shall be
upon his shoulder; and his name shall be

called Wonderful, Counselor, The Mighty God, The Everlasting Father, The Prince of Peace. Of the increase of his government and peace there shall be no end, upon the throne of David, and upon his kingdom, to order it, and to establish it with justice and with righteousness from henceforth even forever. The zeal of the LORD of hosts will perform this" (Isaiah 9:6, 7).

These verses explicitly tell us that the One upon whom the government will rest, and through whom justice, peace and righteousness will come to the earth, is at the same time both man and God. As a child He is born to the nation Israel. This conveys emphatically the Messiah's humanity. At the same time, however, He is also recognized to be God, for He is a Son given by God. This child and Son is called "The Mighty God". He is called "Wonderful, Counselor . . . The Everlasting Father, The Prince of Peace."

Jeremiah joins Isaiah to insist that the Messiah is God in flesh, "Behold, the days come, saith the LORD, that I will raise unto David a righteous Branch, and a King shall reign and prosper, and shall execute justice and righteousness in the earth. In his

days Judah shall be saved, and Israel shall
dwell safely; and this is his name whereby
he shall be called, THE LORD OUR
RIGHTEOUSNESS" (Jeremiah 23:5, 6).

Without question, this statement refers to the Messiah who will be from the
lineage of David. As King of Israel, He will
bring justice, righteousness and peace to the
earth. Who will accomplish all of this? According to this portion of God's Word, He
will be the righteous Branch of David (Messiah) — *Jehovah-Tsidkenu,* "THE LORD
OUR RIGHTEOUSNESS."   Since God
makes it absolutely clear that there are no
gods beside Himself, how can we understand His calling His servant, the Messiah,
God? It can only be understood when we
see that this Son of God, this righteous
Branch, is indeed God.

The Messiah is Eternal

In a limited sense, some of the qualities of God are exhibited in His creation,
particularly in mankind. There are, however, many characteristics which are resi-
dent only in God himself. Eternality is
among those attributes ascribed to God
alone. Unlike man, or any substance in the

universe, God not only exists forever, but He has no beginning – He always was. God revealed Himself to Moses as "I AM THAT I AM" (Exodus 3:14) – a declaration designed to show His awe-smitten servant the past, present and future existence of His divine Person. He just is! Likewise, there are many other passages in the Old and New Testaments which inform us that before anything was brought into existence, God was there.

With this in mind, we turn our attention to teachings which touch on the Messiah's preexistence. Not only was He to be born as a human being at some historical point in time, but also, according to Micah, the Messiah (Son of God) is from everlasting. In chapter 5, verse 2 of his message, this Jewish prophet writes: "But thou, Bethlehem Ephrathah, though thou be little among the thousands of Judah, yet out of thee shall he come forth unto me that is to be ruler in Israel, whose goings forth have been from of old, from everlasting." The birthplace of the coming Prince was foretold centuries before He made His appearance. Messiah would come to the human scene not simply as the product of a virgin's womb, but emerging from the regions of eternity where he existed from everlasting.

It is important to understand that both the Old and New Testaments shatter the concept of the physical birth of Jesus as his beginning — nowhere in the Scriptures is this taught. Likewise, the Bible never gives credence to the claim that Mary is the mother of God, since God never had a birth — He has always been. What the New Testament does reveal, in conjunction with the Old Testament, is that God manifested Himself in flesh as a human being. Mary was the Jewish woman chosen to bring forth this One who was God incarnate — the Son of God.

The Messiah Receives Worship

God alone is the legitimate recipient of worship. He forbids directing worship to any other being or object in heaven or on earth. In Psalm 118:8 we are instructed in this regard. "It is better to trust in the LORD than to put confidence in man." Even more dogmatic is the Prophet Jeremiah. He quotes God as saying: "Cursed be the man that trusteth in man, and maketh flesh his arm, and whose heart departeth from the LORD . . . Blessed is the man who trusteth in the LORD, and whose hope the

THE MESSIAH RECEIVES WORSHIP

LORD is" (Jeremiah 17:5, 7).

Yet in other portions of Scripture we find the Messiah receiving worship. David makes this clear in the second Psalm. He identifies the Messiah as the Son of God and then instructs that the Messiah-King is to be worshipped (verse 12). This could be shocking to the true believer — unless he understands the *tri-unity* of God. Then the admonition to "Kiss [worship] the Son . . . " is both logical and scriptural.

God makes it abundantly clear that His Son, the Messiah, is entitled to receive worship, and He therefore is God. If this were not the case, the only alternative would be to believe that God, who warns us not to reverence man, is contradicting Himself by telling us to do so. Of course, God is not contradicting Himself, but is driving home the point once more: The Messiah is God.

WHEN

GOD

BECOMES

MAN

GOD IN HUMAN FORM

Chapter Four

When God
Becomes Man

AS we have seen, the New Testament
teaching that God became flesh is not re-
stricted to one portion of the Sacred Vol-
ume. Not only are there many statements
supporting this doctrine in the Old Testament, but there are several instances of
theophanies (appearances of God in flesh)
in the Old Testament as well.

In Genesis, chapters 18 and 19, God
appeared before Abraham, the father of
the nation of Israel. This appearance took
the form of a human being. Moses makes
careful note of this manifestation of God
as a man. In verse 1 of chapter 18, the Lord
appeared to Abraham. In verse 2 we are
told Abraham looked upon Him. In verse
14, while addressing Abraham, the Lord
said of Himself, "Is anything too hard for
the LORD? At the time appointed I will
return unto thee . . . ." Verses 16 through
33 record the boldness of Abraham as he
pleaded with the Lord for the deliverance
of his nephew, Lot, and the members of

his family. This man, before whom Abraham was interceding, was called "the Lord" no less than nine times. Further examination verifies that this individual was God in human form. He was the One who chose Abraham. He was the One who dealt severely with Sodom and Gomorrah. He was the One who made the final decision not to destroy the cities if ten righteous people could be found there. The proof cannot be denied: This man, who was present in flesh and had eaten physical food with Abraham was none other than the true, living God.

This phenomenon occurs again when God, in the form of a man, paid a nocturnal visit to Jacob on the bank of the Jabbok. In this encounter Jacob came face to face with God (Genesis 32:24-32). The occasion was significant because it was here that Jacob's name was changed to Israel. Of much greater importance, however, is the fact that God met the patriarch robed in humanity.

A brief pause to examine this episode will be instructive. Jacob actually wrestled with a man, eventually having his thigh dislocated by his heavenly adversary. The weary combatant exclaimed that this man was unmistakably God. He memorialized the encounter by calling the place "Peniel", which means "the Face of God" and exclaimed: " . . . I have seen God face to face, and my life is preserved" (Genesis 32:30). So great was the significance of the event that the impact lingers with us today. Scripture states, "Therefore the children of Israel eat not of the sinew which shrank, which is upon the hollow of the thigh, unto this day: because he touched the hollow of Jacob's thigh in the sinew that shrank" (Genesis 32:32). As a reminder of Jacob's meeting with God, Kosher butchers will not handle or sell the sinew of an animal.

Moses himself was not to be denied one of these awesome experiences — he too came face to face with his God. It was Moses who related that no man can see God and live (Exodus 33:20). Still, God did appear to him in the form of "the angel of the LORD" who spoke to Moses out of a bush that burned but was not consumed (Exodus 3:2). A closer look at this text reveals that "the angel of the LORD" was in fact the Lord himself. Verse 4 clarifies the matter. " . . . when the *LORD* saw that he turned aside to see, *God* called unto him out of the midst of the bush . . . ." Jehovah commanded Moses to remove his sandals because the spot where he stood was holy. This person who appeared to Moses identifies Himself clearly in verse 6: "I am the God of thy father, the God of Abraham, the God of Isaac, and the God of Jacob. And Moses hid his face; for he was afraid to look upon God."

Moses obviously believed that he was standing in the presence of God Almighty. In this theophany, Jehovah revealed Himself in a form Moses could view without risking death. He was not viewing the essence of God, which would have caused his demise, but a manifestation which caused him to recognize his visitor as Deity. In "the angel of the LORD" — God in the form of man — Moses saw the Lord.

These incidents provide convincing evidence to make the God-man concept rational and logical. Thus, when we are confronted with the statement that God became a man, we accept it as the natural culmination of what these Old Testament examples prefigured.

Consider Isaiah 7:14: "Therefore the Lord himself shall give you a sign; Behold, the virgin shall conceive, and bear a son, and shall call his name Immanuel [God with us]." Immanuel, prophesied through the prophet, would be to us what "the angel of the LORD" had been to Moses, Jacob and Abraham — God in human form. This is the essence of the truth exposed in these experiences; the heart of what God said with respect to the long view of the Messiah's personal ministry in our midst. The message is clear and vital to each of us:

> *God would one day appear garbed in flesh.* "I have seen God face to face."
> *He would enter time as the promised Deliverer.* "I have come down to deliver them . . . ."
> *Jehovah would, in the Messiah, ultimately reign.* " . . . and the government shall be upon his shoulder, and his name shall be called Wonderful, Counselor, The Mighty God, The Everlasting Father, The Prince of Peace."

By prestating His intent in Old Testament prophecies and illustrations, God did not drive a divisive wedge between the two Testaments. Rather He established a basis for what He revealed in the New Testament. In other words, what we have in the whole of the Bible is not discord, but perfect harmony. The New Testament exposes what we were taught by the Old Testament to expectantly await. Jesus Christ, Messiah of Israel, came as God in flesh. He appeared as Deliverer and Redeemer of Jew and Gentile alike. In a yet future day, He will reign as King.

A Final Word

We have shared together a number of momentous considerations — truths that will liberate our minds if we are willing to put off restrictive, tradition-bound beliefs and view the Scriptures objectively. God's Book, Old Testament and New, does teach that the omnipotent Lord is a triune personality.   In this,   biblical Judaism (through the Old Testament Scriptures) and biblical Christianity are in precise agreement.

Bible-believing Christians are not polytheists, but their doctrine is as truly monotheistic as is biblical Judaism. In fact, without an understanding of the *tri-unity* of God, one would be at a loss to explain much of the teaching of the Old Testament.

The crux of the entire matter finally settles in an explanation of the impact of the life and ministry of Jesus Christ. For over two millennia He has captivated hearts and dominated history. To be perfectly candid, how can we explain Him, apart from the fact that He is God?

BRIDGING

THE

GAP...

THE

MESSIAHSHIP

OF

JESUS

Chapter Five

Bridging the Gap...
The Messiahship of Jesus

Two thousand years ago, Jesus of Nazareth claimed that He fulfilled the prophecies of the MESSIAH found in the Hebrew Scriptures. He said:

". . . these are the words which I spoke unto you . . . that all things must be fulfilled, which were written in the law of Moses, and in the prophets, and in the psalms concerning me."

Luke 24:44

Did He fulfill the scriptural prophecies of MESSIAH? "MESSIAH" comes from the Hebrew word which means in its verb form "to anoint" – "the act of anointing." It is also found in the noun form referring to the one who has been "anointed." This is seen in such passages as Psalm 2:2, where David writes concerning the kings and the rulers rebelling against the LORD and the LORD'S Anointed (Messiah); also in Daniel 9:25, 26 where the prophet, under inspiration of God, states the MESSIAH (Anointed), who is the prince, shall be cut off.

Scripturally, the concept of "anointing" makes reference to "consecrating"—setting one apart for a specific ministry of God.

The prophets, kings and priests of the Nation of Israel were "consecrated"; that is, they were "anointed" for the ministries for which they had been set apart. A systematic study of MESSIAH in the Old Testament reveals that there would be a specific "Anointed One" of God — God's Servant, who would come and deliver Israel and the Jewish people. This one would be "anointed" by God to perform a specific ministry upon the earth.

Down through history, many Jewish people were and still are looking for a time when they will experience peace, justice, and righteousness upon the face of the earth — a time when they will have inner peace, as well as peace with mankind.

The Hebrew Scriptures teach that this righteousness, justice, and peace will come through an INDIVIDUAL. This INDIVIDUAL is recognized as the Servant of God, the "Anointed One" of God.

The Bible foretells that He will come as a victorious KING to reign and rule over Israel, and the whole earth. At the same time, however, these Scriptures teach of a suffering SERVANT, who, as the "Anointed One" of God, would pay sin's penalty for Israel and the rest of the world.

It is no wonder that many of the ancient rabbis wrote in the Jewish Talmud of two Messiahs who would appear on the stage of human history. Studying intensely as they did, it was obvious to them that not only would there be a Messiah whom they called Messiach Ben David (Messiah, son of David) who would reign and rule as David did, but that there also would be a Messiah whom they called Messiach Ben Joseph (Messiah, son of Joseph) for He would suffer as Joseph suffered.

Comparing the New Testament with the Old Testament, it is clear that Jesus fulfills both aspects of the Messiah — victorious King and suffering Servant.

The Holy Scriptures are bursting with prophecies concerning this "Anointed One" of God. In fact, there are hundreds of prophecies which establish accurate and vivid details enabling one to recognize the

Messiah. More than three hundred of these messianic prophecies were fulfilled in the historical person, Jesus, at what is commonly called His First Coming or Advent.

Some seeking to prove the validity of the messiahship of Jesus have mathematically demonstrated that Jesus, and only Jesus, fulfills all of the messianic prophecies. Josh McDowell in his book, "Evidence That Demands A Verdict," in the chapter dealing with messianic prophecies, after showing their fulfillment in the person of Jesus, points out that it is unthinkable that all of these precise events happened coincidentally. On page 175, he quotes Peter Stoner, who upon examining only forty-eight of more than three hundred messianic prophecies, wrote as follows: "We find the chance that any one man fulfilled all forty-eight prophecies to be one in 10^{157}." This would mean that the probability of only forty-eight prophecies out of several hundred to be fulfilled in one person is the number "10" with one-hundred-fifty-seven "0's" after it to "1." Others have said that if in this group of prophecies there appeared the prediction of both "when" and "where" the Messiah would be born, the probability of all of this occurring in one person goes beyond our ability to express it in figures. Not only have these prophecies concerning the Messiah been fulfilled in the person of Jesus — but literally scores more have been fulfilled in detail.

One cannot honestly escape the truth that Jesus is the Messiah. Listed below are selected messianic prophecies and their interpretation providing the evidence for the messiahship of Jesus. These were chronologically arranged by David Levy in his article on messianic prophecies which appeared in the October/November 1975 issue of the magazine, ISRAEL MY GLORY.

PROPHECY AND FULFILLMENT

MESSIAH'S PLACE OF BIRTH

Micah 5:2 - But thou, Bethlehem Ephrathah, though thou be little among the thousands of Judah, yet out of thee shall he come forth unto me that is to be ruler in Israel; whose goings forth have been from of old, from everlasting.

**Matthew 2:1 - Now when Jesus
was born in Bethlehem of
Judaea in the days of Herod
,the king . . . . (cf. Luke 2:4-7)**

Interpretation: The chief priest and scribes
knew where Messiah would be born: "And
they said unto him, In Bethlehem of
Judaea: for thus it is written by the prophet, and thou Bethlehem, in the land of
Juda, art not the least among the princes
of Juda; for out of thee shall come
a Governor, that shall rule my people
Israel" (Matthew 2:5, 6). Notice, they clearly stated that Messiah would come from
Bethlehem in the land of Judah. All the
Jewish people in Messiah's day knew He
was to come from Bethlehem: "Hath not
the scripture said, That Christ cometh of
the seed of David, and out of the town of
Bethlehem, where David was?" (John 7:42).
Bethlehem means "house of bread", and
Messiah is our "Bread of Life". Also notice
that the One born is to be a "ruler in Israel"
(Micah 5:2), who is deity, "whose goings
forth have been from of old, from everlasting." This prophecy clearly shows that Messiah who was born in Bethlehem, pre-exist-
ed (before He was born): therefore, He is

divine.

MESSIAH'S MANNER OF BIRTH

Isaiah 7:14 - Therefore the Lord himself shall give you a sign: Behold, a virgin shall conceive, and bear a son, and shall call his name Immanuel.

> **Matthew 1:18 - Now the birth of Jesus Christ was on this wise: When as his mother Mary was espoused to Joseph, before they came together, she was found with child of the Holy Ghost (cf. Luke 1:26-35).**

Interpretation:

Sign — The context shows that the sign would not be just for Ahaz, who had rejected the idea of a sign from God, but was to be for the "house of David", which Ahaz did represent during this time (Isaiah 7:13).

Virgin — (Hebrew "Almah" - to conceal) The word "Almah" is used in Genesis 24: 43; Exodus 2:8; Psalm 68:25; Song of Solomon 1:3; 6:8; Proverbs 30:19. The context of these passages favor the translation of "virgin" for Almah. In the third century B.C. (long before Christ's birth),

Jewish translators of the Septuagint render-
ed the word "Almah" with a Greek term
for virgin "parthenos". Matthew 1:23, quot-
ing Isaiah 7:14 from the Septuagint, used
the same term "parthenos".

Rashi (1040 - 1105 A.D.), the great mid-
ieval Jewish commentator, known for his
opposition to Christianity stated, "Behold,
the 'Almah' shall conceive and bare a son
and shall call his name Immanuel. This
means that our Creator shall be with us.
And this is the sign: the one who will conceive is a girl (naarah), who never in her
life has had intercourse with any man. Upon this one shall the Holy Spirit have power." (Buksbazen, Isaiah the Prophet, p. 150,
Vol. II).

Immanuel — the word literally means "God
with us". The word sets forth both His
deity and His humanity. Other Scriptures
bring out this same concept (Isaiah 9:6;
John 1:14; Philippians 2:5-11). Therefore,
the child born of a virgin is "God with us",
our Messiah.

MESSIAH'S TIME OF BIRTH

Genesis 49:10 - The sceptre
shall not depart from Judah,

nor a lawgiver from between
his feet, until Shiloh come; and
unto him shall the gathering of
the people be.

> **Galatians 4:4 - But when the
> fulness of the time was come,
> God sent forth his Son, made
> of a woman, made under the
> law (cf Matthew 1:23; Luke 3:
> 33).**

Interpretation:

Shiloh — Rabbis have interpreted this to
mean Messiah (the Prince of Peace) for centuries. Some want to say this was fulfilled
in David, but this is impossible since there
was no actual ruler from Judah until David
ruled. But the verse says that there was rule
in Judah before Shiloh was to come; therefore, David could not have fulfilled the
prophecy.

Sceptre and lawgiver shall not depart —
Sceptre has always been interpreted to
mean "tribal-rod or staff of office", which
was the ensign of authority. The idea is that
Judah should retain both its tribal distinctness and separate authority until Shiloh
(the Messiah) had appeared.

Lawgiver shall not depart — The legal authority of Judah to make laws and judge shall remain until Messiah has come. In 70 A.D., Judah lost both her "sceptre" (tribal distinctness) and "lawgiver" (legal authority to make laws). Therefore, Shiloh (Messiah) must have come before 70 A.D. Jesus had to be the One who fulfilled this prophecy and is the Messiah.

Daniel 9:25, 26 — Know therefore and understand, that from the going forth of the commandment to restore and to build Jerusalem unto the Messiah the Prince shall be seven weeks, and threescore and two weeks: the street shall be built again, and the wall, even in troublous times. And after threescore and two weeks shall Messiah be cut off, but not for himself: and the people of the prince that shall come shall destroy the city and the sanctuary; and the end thereof shall be with a flood, and unto the end of the war desolations are determined.

Interpretation: Daniel 9:25 - From the commandment to rebuild the City of Jerusalem (which took place under the edict of Artaxerxes on March 14, 445 B.C., by our corresponding calendar date), until Messiah's presenting of Himself would be 69 prophetical weeks of years (which would

come to a total of 173,880 days — this is
based upon the fact that the Scriptures
speak of a year as having 360 days, or each
month containing thirty days — 69 x 360
equals 173,880 days). Gen. 7:11, 8:4, 7:24,
8:3; Rev. 13:4-7, 12:6.

    445 B.C. to 32 A.D. is   476 years
        (B.C. 1 to A.D. 1 is one year)
    476 x 365 days   173,740 days
    add for leap years   116 days
        (3 less in 4 centuries)
    March 14 to April 6   24 days (incl.)
                        173,880 total days
        (Sir Robert Anderson's dates)

No matter how you figure the dates, the
Messiah had to come before the destruction
of Jerusalem (McDowell, EVIDENCE
THAT DEMANDS A VERDICT, p. 181).

Daniel 9:26 - At the end of the 69 weeks,
Messiah will be "cut off" (killed), but not
for Himself (for the world). The city (Jerusalem) and the sanctuary (Temple) will be
destroyed by the prince (Titus of Rome).
This took place 40 years after Messiah's
crucifixion in 70 A.D. Therefore, Messiah
had to come while the Temple was standing
before 70 A.D.

MESSIAH'S RECEPTION

Isaiah 53:3 - He is despised and rejected of men; a man of sorrows, and acquainted with grief; and we hid as it were our faces from him; he was despised, and we esteemed him not.

John 1:11 - He came unto his own, and his own received him not (cf. John 5:43; 7:5).

Interpretation: He was despised (felt contempt and scorn) and rejected (shunned) by men. The word for "men" (Hebrew ishim) is a reference not to ordinary men, but to men of stature and standing, or rank. They despised and rejected or felt contempt for Him and shunned Him.

And we hid our faces — The Jewish people and others have loathed to look at Messiah whom they have hated immensely. For hundreds of years His name was not mentioned among the Jewish people. The Hebrew name for Jesus, "Yeshua" (Saviour), has been deliberately distorted into "Yeshu", the initial letters which were supposed to spell out a Hebrew sentence which means, "Let his name and his memory be blotted out." Notice that "He was despised" is repeated twice to emphasize the intensity of man's hatred for Him. (Buksbazen, "The Prophet Isaiah", p. 416).

"Esteemed him not" — It means that men estimated the Messiah as "a nothing", or less than a person when He came to them.

MESSIAH'S SUFFERING

Isaiah 53:3 - . . . a man of sorrows, and acquainted with grief . . . .

> **Matthew 26:38 - Then saith he unto them, My soul is exceeding sorrowful, even unto death . . . .**

> **Matthew 27:30, 31 - And they spit upon him, and took the reed and smote him on the head. And after that they had mocked him, they took the robe off from him, and put his own raiment on him, and led him away to crucify him.**

Interpretation: Sorrow (Hebrew Machoboth. Lit. "affliction") — Sorrow means affliction or grief, which could either be physical or spiritual. Messiah felt the maladies of His people with a keen personal sensitivity.

Grief (Lit. "with sickness") — Not that He, by nature, had a sickly body; but that the wrath instigated by sin, and the zeal of self-sacrifice, burnt like a fire in His soul and body, so that even if He had not died a violent death, He would have succumbed to the force of destruction that was innate in His humanity because of the consequences of our sin which He bore and His own self-consuming conflict with them (Delitzsch, "Isaiah", Vol. II, p. 314).

Isaiah 53:4 - Surely he hath borne our griefs, and carried our sorrows . . . .

> **Matthew 8:17 - That it might be fulfilled which was spoken by Esaias the prophet, saying, Himself took our infirmities, and bare our sicknesses.**

nterpretation: "Borne our griefs and carried our sorrows" is literally "borne our sickness and carried our pain." "Borne and carry" have the idea "to take upon oneself, and carry it as one's own". Messiah bore them in His own person, that He might deliver us from them. Therefore, He became our substitute, suffering for our sins. This suffering was expiatory and vicarious in nature. The word "bear" (Hebrew "Nass") is also connected with the sacrifice of expiation in Leviticus 5:1, 17; 16:22; 20:19, 20 (Buksbazen, "The Prophet Isaiah" Vol. II, p. 417):

Isaiah 53:4 - . . . yet we did esteem him stricken, smitten of God, and afflicted.

> **Matthew 27:41, 43 - Likewise also the chief priests mocking him, with the scribes and elders, said . . . He trusted in God; let him deliver him now, if he will have him, for he said, I am the Son of God.**

Interpretation: Stricken (Hebrew "Nagua") — refers to a disease like leprosy.

Smitten of God — divine retribution for a heinous sin.

Afflicted — refers to being afflicted by punishment for one's crime (Buksbazen, "The Prophet Isaiah", Vol. II, p. 417).

All of these terms describe the terrible consequences of our sin upon the Messiah when he suffered for us.

Isaiah 53:5 -   But he was wounded for our transgressions, he was bruised for our iniquities, the chastisement of our peace was upon him; and with his stripes we are healed.

> 1 Peter 2:24 - Who his own self bare our sins in his own body on the tree, that we being dead to sins, should live unto righteousness: by whose stripes ye were healed (cf. Matthew 27: 26, 29; 1 Peter 3:18; Colossians 1:20).

Interpretation: "But he" — Emphatic assertion that he suffered not for His own sins, but for those of His people.

"Wounded" (Hebrew "Mecholal") — Literally means "He was pierced". Isaiah describes His actual type of death 700 years before it takes place. He was pierced with thorn (Matthew 27:29), nails (John 20:25), and a spear (John 19:34).

"He was bruised for our iniquities" — Bruised literally means crushed by the heavy load of our sins upon Him.   "For" - He went through this suffering "for" our sin.

"The chastisement of our peace was upon Him" — Literally, "chastisement which secured peace" (Hebrew "Musar Shlomenu"). Forgiveness, to be real, must be obtained at a price. Therefore, Messiah took upon Himself the chastisement or punishment which secures our peace (Buksbazen, "The Prophet Isaiah", Vol. II, p. 418).

"With His stripes we are healed" — By His stripes (vicarious suffering), we may secure peace (shalom), that is complete reconciliation with God. Healing here is the healing of the soul from the sickness of sin (Buksbazen, "The Prophet Isaiah", Vol. II, p. 418).

Isaiah 53:7 - He was oppressed, and he was afflicted, yet he opened not his mouth: he is brought as a lamb to the slaughter, and as a sheep before her shearers is dumb, so he openeth not his mouth.

1 Peter 2:23 - Who, when he was reviled, reviled not again;

when he suffered, he threaten-
ed not; but committed himself to him that judgeth right-
eously (cf. Matthew 26:62-63;
27:12-14).

MESSIAH'S DEATH

Isaiah 53:8 - . . . for he was
cut off out of the land of the
living; for the transgression of
my people was he stricken.

Luke 23:33 - And when they
were come to the place, which
is called Calvary, there they
crucified him . . . .

Interpretation: He was "cut off" or taken
away before His time (cut down like a
flower). Messiah was killed at an early age,
when He was only 33 years old.

Daniel 9:26 - And after threescore and two weeks shall Messiah be cut off, but not for
himself . . . .

Luke 23:33 - And when they
were come to the place . . . called Calvary . . . they crucified him . . . .

Luke 24:26 - Ought not Christ to have suffered these things . . . .

Interpretation: Again this shows clearly that Messiah would be killed at a specific time for mankind. (See interpretation under "Messiah's Time of Birth").

Isaiah 53:12 - . . . he hath poured out his soul unto death . . . .

John 19:30 - . . . It is finished: and he bowed his head, and gave up the ghost.

Interpretation: The Messiah poured out His life unto death at the time of His crucifixion.

MESSIAH'S RESURRECTION

Psalm 16:10 - For thou wilt not leave my soul in Sheol; neither wilt thou suffer thine Holy One to see corruption.

Acts 2:31 - He seeing this before spake of the resurrection of Christ, that his soul was not left in hades, neither his flesh did see corruption.

Interpretation: This prophecy definitely refers to the resurrection of Messiah and cannot refer to David. It speaks of not allowing the "Holy One" (Messiah) to see "corruption" (bodily decay after death) in "sheol" (the grave). David is still in the grave and his body has decayed. Neither was David ever called a "Holy One" (pious one). Therefore, we clearly see from this passage that the Messiah was resurrected after His death.

Isaiah 53:10 - . . . he shall prolong his days.

Interpretation: This refers to Messiah's resurrection. If Messiah has died as is mentioned in this chapter, verses 8 and 9, then the words, "he shall prolong his days" must mean He is resurrected.

SO
WHAT ?

Chapter Six

So What?

For centuries men have thirsted after a utopian society — an era when peace, righteousness, justice and equity would exist for all men. Mankind has feverishly endeavored to purge the world of war, famine and sickness.

Many have put their faith in a progressive, enlightened world, believing that as mankind became more knowledgeable — as he advanced scientifically and technologically — he would naturally turn his vast knowledge and ability toward creating this society. Actually, however, history demonstrates this hope to be false. Instead of progressing toward this utopia, man has been on a continuous decline, morally and spiritually. He has advanced from the individual weaponry of a club to potential total ruination by the atomic bomb — from a moral conviction of absolutes to a philosophy of situation ethics — from societal concern to near total apathy.

Centuries ago, God gave the formula for a perfect age to Israel in the Hebrew Scriptures. Its fulfillment will be found in the Messiah, as recorded in the Old and New Testaments.

This naturally leads to the question, "How does the Messiah deal with the issue of man's ills?" Or, even more important, "What is the ultimate purpose of the Messiah?"

Necessity of Conversion

The historical record of man's dilemma is analogous to that which God has taught concerning the heart of man's problem. Ultimately, man's failure to reach a utopian age is traced to sin — a conscious and unconscious rebellion toward God. Sin is anything which contradicts God's character. It not only involves breaking God's laws, but also includes not doing what He desires of us. It is anything that removes us from harmony with Him.

A salient glance at society reveals sin in every sphere of human experience. A discerning inward examination unmasks the truth that we are all at enmity with God. It is not necessary to be a theologian or religionist to recognize that mankind falls short of the requirements of God.

Both the Old and New Testaments are

very clear and unambiguous in their teaching concerning sin. God declares that there are none righteous — no, not one — all have sinned against Him (Ecclesiastes 7:20, Psalm 14:1-3, Isaiah 64:6, Jeremiah 17:9 and Romans 3:9-10 and 23). It is precisely for this reason that God demands *conversion*. Both the Hebrew and Greek words translated *conversion* mean *turning from one thing to another*.

Conversion has no bearing on one's birthright, but rather affects one's personal relationship with God. Contextually, conversion refers to man's turning to God and away from his present condition of sin. Obviously then, it is erroneous to say that a Jewish person becomes a Gentile, or a Gentile becomes Jewish, when accepting Jesus as Saviour and becoming *converted*.

The biblical teaching on this subject is unobscured. Doctor Luke, in his historical account of the early church testifies to this truth in the Acts of the Apostles: "And being brought on their way by the church, they passed through Phoenicia and Samaria, declaring the *conversion of the Gentiles;* and they caused great joy unto all the brethren" (Acts 15:3).

Obviously, Luke was not implying

that the Gentiles had become Jews, but
rather that they had turned from their life
of paganism to the true, living God by accepting Jesus as Messiah. One only needs to
read the context of the chapter to understand his statement.

Conversion is not unique to the New
Testament, for in the Old Testament Israel
was entreated to be *converted.* King David,
in his penitential prayer, declared his concern for his people: "Then will I teach
transgressors thy ways; and sinners *shall be
converted unto thee"* (Psalm 51:13). Likewise, Isaiah makes a similar statement concerning the conversion of the Jewish people
in Isaiah 6:10. David and Isaiah were not
exhorting Jews to become Gentiles, but
rather to turn to the true, living God and
away from their lives of sin. This is what
Isaiah had in mind when he said, "All we
like sheep have gone astray; we have turned
every one to his own way . . . . "
(Isaiah 53:6).

Since we are all sinners, and have all
gone astray, all must be *converted.*

Necessity of a Circumcized Heart

The Bible teaches that every person,
both Jew and Gentile, must have circum-

cision performed on the heart. Obviously, God is not speaking of literal, physical circumcision; He is referring to a spiritual, internal change.

Man's predicament is vividly demonstrated in Isaiah's statement: "But your iniquities have separated between you and your God, and your sins have hidden his face from you, that he will not hear" (Isaiah 59:2). This presents an insurmountable problem. Since all men have hearts that are in opposition to God, how can one convert? How can one turn to God from his present position?

The answer once again is found in the Bible. A transformation must take place within, which will permit man to have an intimate relationship with the true and living God. The only possible solution to man's dilemma is found as God himself makes the heart *kosher* (pure, fit and clean).

On three occasions the Apostle Paul states that the only way to have a true relationship and fellowship with God is to undergo the internal operation of having the heart circumcized. God is not referring to the heart which maintains life support by pumping blood throughout the body, but to the very core of man's total being, all that he is — emotions, intellect and will.

In his epistle to the church in Rome, Paul emphasized this principle. In chapter 2, starting at verse 17 and continuing through the end of the chapter, he unfolds the truth about the natural-born Jew. In verses 28 and 29, Paul explains what it takes for this natural Jew to be a Jew as God intended him to be. He says that it is only as one experiences *circumcision of the heart:* "For he is not a Jew who is one outwardly; neither is that circumcision which is outward in the flesh; But he is a Jew who is one inwardly; and circumcision is that of the heart, in the spirit and not in the letter; whose praise is not of men, but of God." Paul in this passage, as well as in Philippians 3:3 and Colossians 2:11, reveals that *circumcision of the heart* is synonymous with new birth, regeneration, becoming a new creation.

This doctrine is not only found in the New Testament, for *circumcision of the heart* originated with the nation of Israel in the Old Testament. It was this truth that Jesus drove home to Nicodemus, as recorded in John's Gospel in chapter 3. Nicodemus, a Jewish leader and teacher apparently searching for the truth, came to

Jesus by night. Jesus minced no words with Nicodemus as He immediately told him what was necessary if he wished to enter the kingdom of God: "Verily, verily, I say unto thee, Except a man be *born again*, he cannot see the kingdom of God" (verse 3). Surprisingly, Jesus seemed to be critical of Nicodemus. After he heard what was required to enter into the kingdom of God, Nicodemus was perplexed. He did not understand how a person could be born a second time. Jesus' response was, "Art thou a teacher of Israel, and knowest not these things?" (verse 10). In essence, Jesus was stating that this teaching of new birth should not have confounded Nicodemus, since he was a teacher of all Israel.

At this time two major facts must be pointed out, for the significance of this event is momentous! First, Jesus had not yet died; and second, the New Testament had not yet been penned. It is the conviction of many that the belief in the new birth, or a regeneration experience, is synonymous with the death, burial and resurrection of Jesus as recorded in the New Testament. While this is true, it must be asked: "What was Jesus referring to, because it is obvious He expected Nicodemus to understand what He was talking about?" The only possible explanation is that the Old Testament revelation to the nation of Israel had also taught this doctrine called *new birth* or *regeneration*. Since Nicodemus was a teacher of Israel, he should not have been caught unaware of this truth.

Today, we have an advantage. We have the completed revelation of God — both the Old and New Testaments.

Centuries ago, Augustine said, "The Old Testament is revealed in the New Testament, and the New Testament is concealed in the Old Testament."

In light of the New Testament, one can now go back to the Old Testament and see that which is concealed, particularly the teaching concerning a *circumcized heart*.

Israel's prophets promulgated the message that God insisted upon a circumcized heart. Moses, Jeremiah and Ezekiel not only revealed this truth but arduously warned Israel of the consequences if they did not heed God's commandment. Moses taught that the remedy for life was through the circumcision of the heart (Deuteronomy 10:16, 30:6). Jeremiah exhorted the Israelites to circumcize their hearts to escape God's fury because of the evil of their doings (Jeremiah 4:4). Ezekiel also unveils the necessity for a new heart (Ezekiel 11:19, 18:31, 36:25-27).

There is no doubt that Jesus was implying that the new birth (circumcision of the heart) should have been understood, and that it was imperative for the Jew as well as for the Gentile, if indeed they desired to enter the kingdom of God.

Necessity of Entering into the New Covenant

Behold, the days come, saith the Lord, that I will make a NEW COVENANT with the house of Israel, and with the house of Judah, Not according to the covenant that I made with their fathers in the day that I took them by the hand to bring them out of the land of Egypt, which, my covenant, they broke, although I was an husband unto them, saith the Lord; But this shall be the covenant that I will make with the house of Israel: After those days, saith the Lord, I WILL PUT MY LAW IN THEIR INWARD PARTS, AND WRITE IT IN THEIR HEARTS, and will be their God, and they shall be my people.   Jeremiah 31:31-33

In the days of Jeremiah, God promised Israel that a day would come when He would work in the hearts of His people, unlike the external law covenant given through Moses. This would be accomplished through the New Covenant which He would make with Israel.

One may search diligently through the entire Old Testament, from Genesis to Malachi, and not find the fulfillment of this New Covenant. It is only as one reads the progressive revelation of God in the New Testament that the fulfillment of the New Covenant is found.

Much to the surprise of many, the first book of the New Testament, the Gospel according to Matthew, is unequivocally Jewish. While this may be new to some, it really should not be thought of as strange — for it was written by a Jewish writer to Jewish people about the Jewish Messiah and Saviour of the world. There are scores of Old Testament Scriptures quoted throughout. Even a brief survey of this book undeniably reveals Jesus to fulfill the messianic prophecies of the Old Testament Scriptures.

It is within this context that the fulfillment of Jeremiah's prophecy concerning the New Covenant is found.

Jesus, a Jew himself, was fulfilling the law by observing the Jewish feast of Passover with his Jewish disciples. Matthew records this event, which is commonly referred to as The Lord's Supper: "And as they were eating, Jesus took bread, and blessed it, and broke it, and gave it to the disciples, and said, Take, eat; this is my body. And he took the cup, and gave thanks, and gave it to them, saying, Drink ye all of it; For this is my blood of the *new testament* (covenant) which is shed for many for the remission of sins" (Matthew 26:26-28).

Since we are removed from this historical event by over nineteen hundred years, special care must be used in interpreting it. However, by placing ourselves in the sandals of the disciples, we can better understand what Jesus meant by this statement. Surely we must rule out the belief that the disciples actually ate the physical body and drank the literal blood of Jesus. Obviously, this could not be so, since He was very much alive and participating in the event Himself.

A closer look clearly reveals that this was a symbolic act, even as Passover itself was. The disciples knew that the Mosaic Covenant, which God made with Israel, was made in blood. They also knew that God had promised Israel a New Covenant. It would not only be inconsistent with the Old Testament Scriptures, but equally unthinkable that the New Covenant would be made without blood. Actually, Jesus was illustrating that as a lamb was sacrificed and its blood shed centuries earlier in behalf of Israel, so He was now going to become the true Passover Lamb by shedding His blood in behalf of Israel and the whole world. There can be no doubt that Jesus was referring to the New Covenant about which Jeremiah spoke.

Conclusion

The quest for a utopia has plagued man ever since the fall out of harmony with God. It will one day become a reality, when mankind becomes reconciled to God through the Messiah. But, what about today? And of a graver nature, what about individual accountability to God — not only for today, but for all eternity? The reconciliation that will one day bring total peace, justice and righteousness to the world can be ours today. It must become ours — yours and mine — if we desire, as Nicodemus did, to enter into the kingdom of heaven.

Not only will you have a full and meaningful life here on earth in relationship and fellowship with God, but you will be assured of eternal life with God as well. This can only come about as we permit the Master Surgeon to circumcize our hearts.

The Apostle Paul wrote that *heart circumcision* is accomplished by the *circumcision of Christ,* the Messiah (Colossians 2:11). When you put your trust in Jesus as your personal Saviour, believing that He was the Lamb sacrificed for your sins, this internal surgery — new birth, circumcision of the heart — is accomplished.

God explicitly states that there is nothing we can do — it must be accomplished by Him. The part you and I play in our salvation is to accept the free gift that God has given us, eternal life through Jesus the Messiah, our Lord: "For the wages of sin is death, but the gift of God is eternal life through Jesus Christ, our Lord" (Rom. 6:23).

While this provision is not a continuation of Judaism, it is consistent with biblical Judaism. The question of supreme importance then, to both Jew and Gentile — to you and me — is: DO WE HAVE CIRCUMCIZED HEARTS? Our decision is a matter of life or death!